LEAVES OF LIFE

Lawrence Ferlinghetti

LEAVES OF LIFE
(First Series)

Fifty Drawings from the Model

Introduction
by
Mendes Monsanto

Ferlinghetti 10/96

CITY LIGHTS BOOKS
San Francisco

A traveling exhibition of the originals of all drawings in this book is available from the Publisher. Galleries and museums please enquire.

Library of Congress Cataloging in Publication Data

Ferlinghetti, Lawrence.
  Leaves of life (first series)

  1. Ferlinghetti, Lawrence.   I. Title.
NC139.F42A4   1983   741.973   83-20850
ISBN 0-87286-154-6 (pbk.)

Printed in the United States of America

CITY LIGHTS BOOKS are published at the City Lights Bookstore, 261 Columbus Avenue, San Francisco 94133.

Introduction

The tragic sense and a sense of joy in life meet in these studies of the human figure by Lawrence Ferlinghetti. The touch is light and sensitive yet curiously profound, for one feels here sometimes that the hand knows something the mind cannot know.

Those connoisseurs of idiocy who pretend there is great emotion and thought in currently fashionable high art will not find Ferlinghetti's drawings to their taste, for there is far too much of both here, disturbing the deep non-objective sleep of the rootless cosmopolitan unpenetrated by either passion or despair.

The high function of art as the locale for fathoming man's fate seems to be mostly forgotten these days. But when one comes to consider that the decay or regression of modern art may be traced to the deterioration or fragmentation of the Image (in every art) we begin to see how valuable drawing such as this may be.

— Mendes Monsanto

July 1983

List of Drawings

1. Untitled (5" x 8½") 1982
2. Perseus (18" x 24") 1981
3. Untitled (19" x 24¾") 1983
4. The Heavy (13¾" x 17") 1983
5. Untitled (18" x 24") 1983
6. Indifference (18" x 24") 1983
7. Untitled (22" x 28") 1982
8. Untitled (5" x 8½") 1982
9. Nude Gesturing (18" x 24") 1982
10. Untitled (12¼" x 14¼" 1983
11. Woman with Faded Face (20" x 23½") 1982
12. Night Class Model (11½" x 19") 1983
13. Dancing Nude (9" x 12") 1982
14. Looking Away (13½" x 17") 1981
15. Untitled (13½" x 17") 1981
16. Untitled (14" x 16½") 1981
17. Kate Careless 1 (15" x 18") 1982
18. Untitled (24" x 36") 1982
19. The Model Revealed (25" x 39¾") 1983
20. Untitled (12" x 17") 1983
21. Person Destroying Self 1 (24" x 36") 1981
22. Person Destroying Self 2 (24" x 36") 1981
23. The Blue Clock (13½" x 17") 1983
24. Intimacy (18" x 24") 1981
25. Untitled (18" x 24") 1983
26. Goodbye, Goodbye (18" x 24") 1983
27. Untitled (15¼" x 17¾") 1983
28. The Couple (18" x 24") 1981
29. Horse & Nude (8" x 11") 1982
30. Study for The Expulsion from Paradise (17¾ x 23¾") 1982
31. The Relationship (18½" x 21¼") 1981
32. Mother & Offspring (20" x 26") 1983
33. A Mystery (13½" x 17") 1983
34. Woman Emergent (36" x 24") 1981
35. Herself Determined (26" x 20") 1983
36. Untitled (12½" x 9½") 1983

37. Kate Careless 2 (24" x 18") 1982
38. Untitled (17" x 13¾") 1983
39. Untitled (18½" x 13¼") 1983
40. A Flood of Feeling (14" x 9½") 1983
41. A Strange Man (24" x 16½") 1983
42. Post-Punk Man (24" x 17¾") 1981
43. Eurydice & Orphée (19" x 12½") 1982
44. Untitled (17¾" x 15") 1981
45. Misapprehension (24" x 18") 1983
46. Untitled (12½" x 9") 1982
47. Running Away from Herself (36" x 24") 1983
48. Lady Bullfighter (17¾" x 12½" 1982
49. Untitled (14" x 10½") 1982
50. True Realities (23¾" x 17¾") 1983

LEAVES
OF
LIFE

1. Untitled (5" x 8½") 1982

3/26/82

2. Perseus (18" x 24") 1981

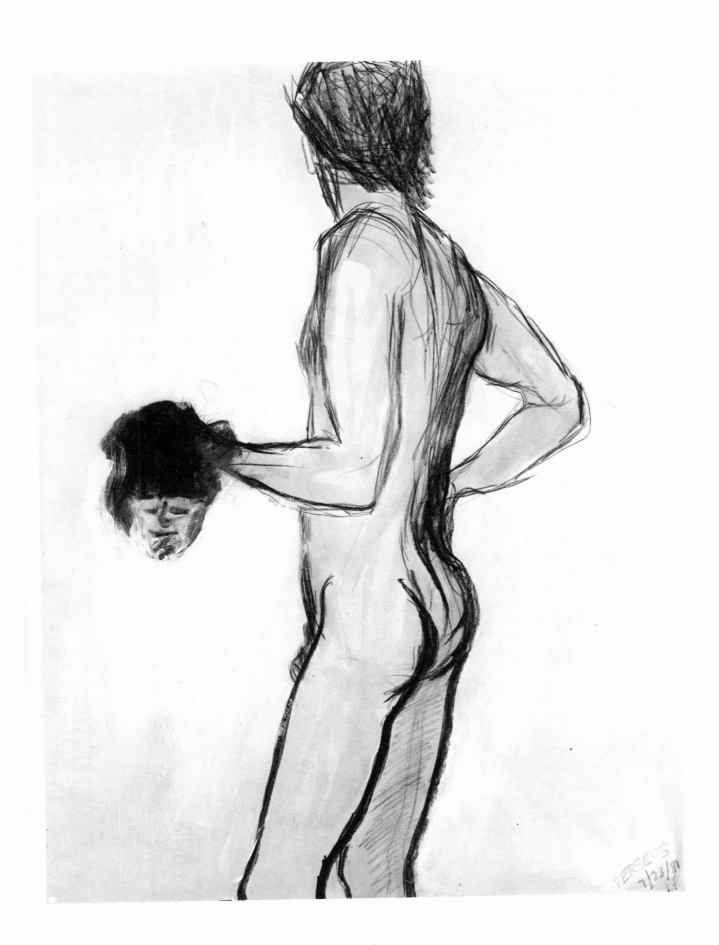

PERSEUS
7/23/81

3. Untitled (19" x 24¾") 1983

Forlocit   2/7/83

4. The Heavy (13¾" x 17") 1983

The HEAVY
4/21/83

5. Untitled (18" x 24") 1983

1/25/83

6. Indifference (18" x 24") 1983

Indifference

LF '85

7. Untitled (22" x 28") 1982

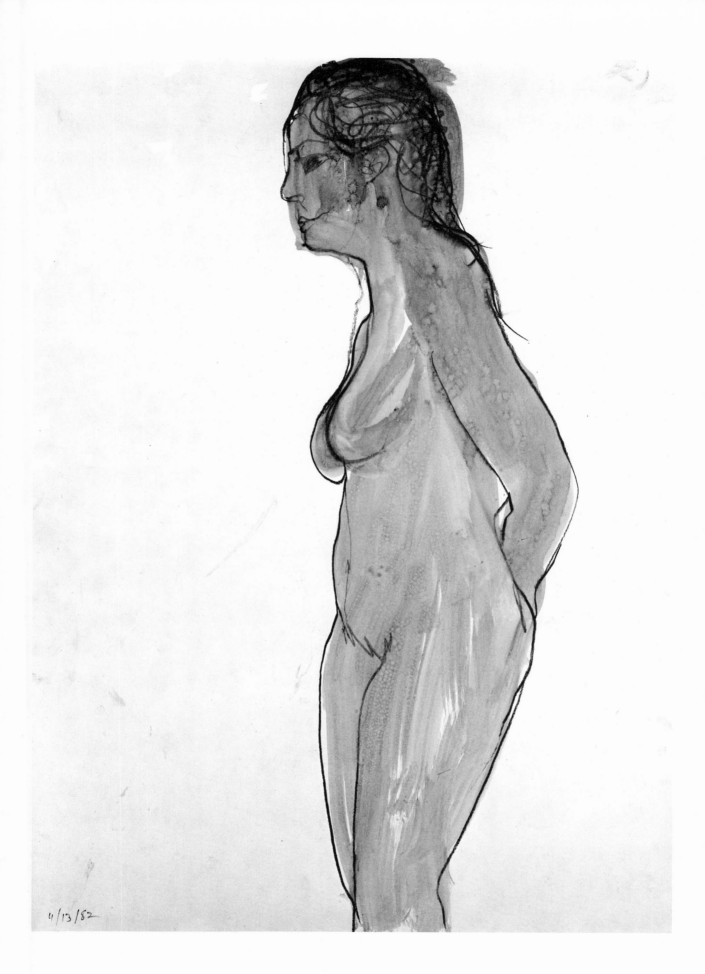

4/13/82

8. Untitled (5" x 8½") 1982

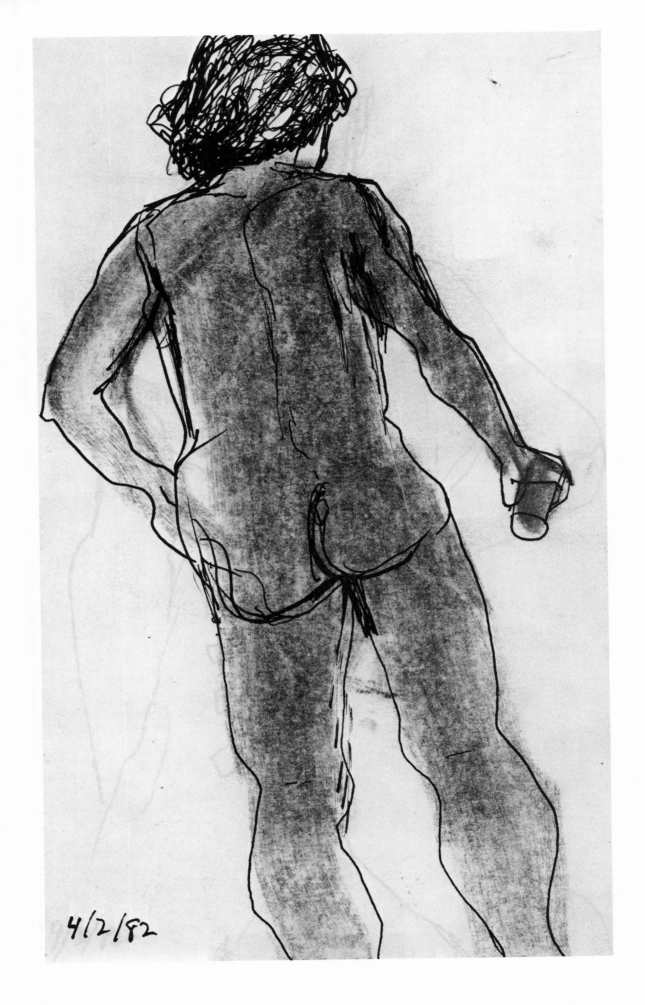

4/2/82

9. Nude Gesturing (18" x 24") 1982

11/30/82

10. Untitled (12¼" x 14¼" 1983

1/23/83

11. Woman with Faded Face (20" x 23½") 1982

2/22/82

12. Night Class Model (11½" x 19") 1983

KF
7/83 Night Class Model

13. Dancing Nude (9" x 12") 1982

4/82

14. Looking Away (13½" x 17") 1981

2/20/81

15. Untitled (13½" x 17") 1981

3-13-81

16. Untitled (14" x 16½") 1981

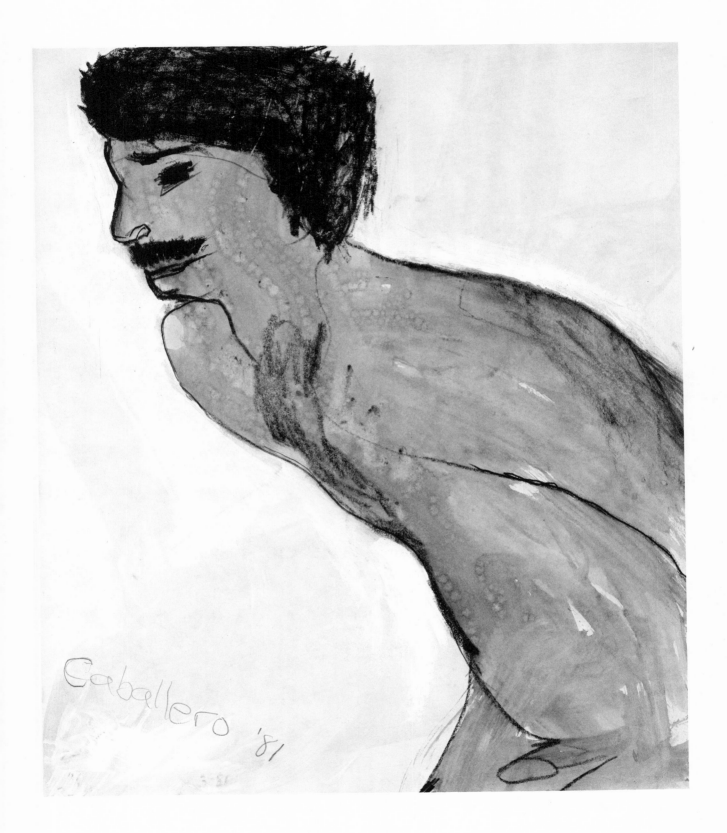
Caballero '81

17. Kate Careless 1 (15" x 18") 1982

Kate Careless

18. Untitled (24" x 36") 1982

LF
1/18/82

19. The Model Revealed (25" x 39¾") 1983

The Model Revealed

Ferlinghetti
7/20/83

20. Untitled (12" x 17") 1983

7/83

21. **Person Destroying Self 1 (24" x 36") 1981**

Ferlinghetti   12/15/81

22. Person Destroying Self 2 (24" x 36") 1981

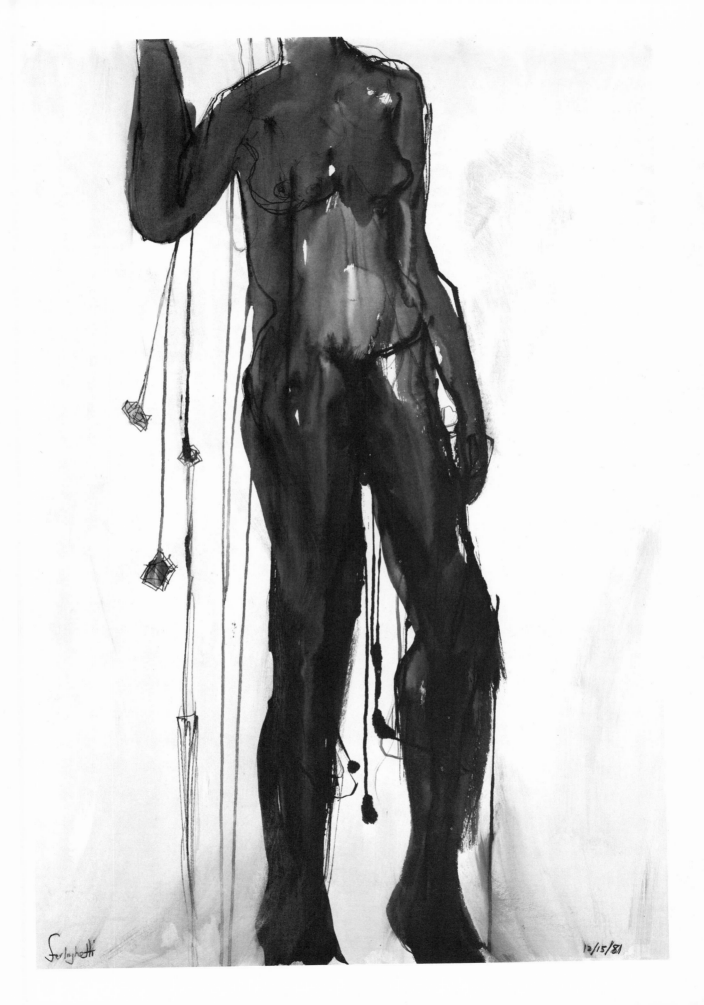

Ferlinghetti   12/15/81

23. **The Blue Clock (13½" x 17") 1983**

8/83

24. Intimacy (18" x 24") 1981

Intimacy....

25. Untitled (18" x 24") 1983

1/23/83

26. Goodbye, Goodbye (18" x 24") 1983

2/7/83

27. Untitled (15¼" x 17¾") 1983

·2/3/83

28. The Couple (18" x 24") 1981

29. Horse & Nude (8" x 11") 1982

30. Study for The Expulsion from Paradise (17¾ x 23¾") 1982

6/9/81

31. The Relationship (18½" x 21¼") 1981

Now I Begin the Buried... South Arms

JF
9/81

32. Mother & Offspring (20" x 26") 1983

7/5/83

33. A Mystery (13½" x 17") 1983

3/18/83 Ferlinghetti

34. Woman Emergent (36" x 24") 1981

WOMAN EMERGENT

Felinghoff.   12/81

35. Herself Determined (26" x 20") 1983

36. Untitled (12½" x 9½") 1983

1/23/83

37. Kate Careless 2 (24" x 18") 1982

38. Untitled (17" x 13¾") 1983

39. Untitled (18½" x 13¼") 1983

LF 2/83

40. A Flood of Feeling (14" x 9½") 1983

A Flood of Feeling

7/20/83

41. A Strange Man (24" x 16½") 1983

A Strange Man

JF'83

42. Post-Punk Man (24" x 17¾") 1981

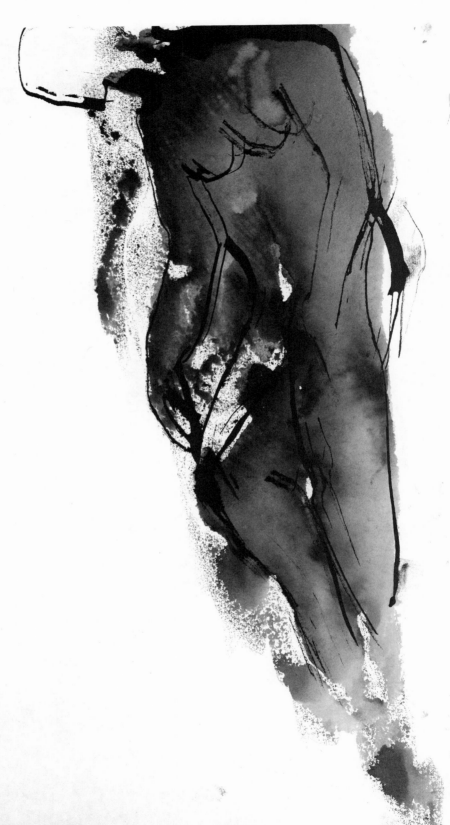

43. Eurydice & Orphée (19" x 12½") 1982

EURYDICE + ORPHÉE — 2/3/92

IF

44. Untitled (17¾″ x 15″) 1981

45. Misapprehension (24" x 18") 1983

Sallybeth

Misapprehension
4/28/83

46. Untitled (12½" x 9") 1982

47. Running Away from Herself (36" x 24") 1983

21/8/83 Turning away from herself

48. Lady Bullfighter (17¾" x 12½" 1982

49. Untitled (14" x 10½") 1982

6/1/82

50. True Realities (23¾" x 17¾") 1983